Immortal Village

Books by Kathryn Rhett

Near Breathing
Souvenir

As editor
Survival Stories: Memoirs of Crisis

Immortal Village

K A T H R Y N   R H E T T

Carnegie Mellon University Press
Pittsburgh 2018

Acknowledgments

Thanks to the editors of the journals where the following poems appeared, with special gratitude to Jane Satterfield:

Bellingham Review: "Night"
Crazyhorse: "Proofs" (as "Proofreader")
The Gettysburg Review: "A Bavaria of the Mind," and "Winter in France"
Grand Street: "Arc," and "I Am the Elder"
The Greensboro Review: "Verge" (as "1974")
Journal of the Motherhood Initiative for Research and Community Involvement (Ontario), included in "Book of Hours," a portfolio selected and introduced by Jane Satterfield: "The Visit," "One a.m.," "Book of Hours," "Dark Wood," "She Falls Back In" (as "Vanish"), "Circumstance," "In the Exhibit," "Trompe L'oeil," "Crown," "Dream," and "I Meant to Speak"
The Ohio Review: "Wedding"
THEthepoetry.com: "In Bed"

Thanks to Cade Leebron, Fred Leebron, Cecily Rhett, Alane Rollings, and Nadine Meyer for reading this manuscript at various stages.

Carnegie Mellon University Press wishes to acknowledge—with great appreciation—the generous support of Courtney and Lisa Cox.

Book design by Kate Martin

Library of Congress Control Number 2017950603
ISBN 978-0-88748-633-3

10 9 8 7 6 5 4 3 2 1

for my family

Contents

PART TWO

Where the lemon blooms,
Where amid the dark leaves
The golden orange glows.

Lines by Goethe, as translated by Donald Culross Peattie,
in *Vence: Immortal Village*

PART ONE

Small Bad Picture

There were bits, when
    wholeness had been wanted.

The pottery in Nicaragua
    must be uniform, admit no flaw, a student told me.

Fragmented into bits, I—
    what woman isn't—contemplate the primitive picture

(large bad picture, wrote Elizabeth Bishop), with its church, clouds,
    volcano, impermeable clumps of tree-matter, all stuck

linked on a flat plane, or pane.
    The painting is a window over my black desk.

("Wait," said the sign over Kafka's desk.)
    In Nicaragua they find our love of flaw so curious—

The Visit

You have to know that I am older now—
my camera in a case,
the kids' school pictures
in my wallet.
I came to see the "Primavera," or
"Allegory of Spring," to be precise,
in the Uffizi Gallery in Florence.

I hadn't seen it for a long time,
except in books
and so I stood near
for a while, ignoring tour groups.
I'd paid my money, and just to see
the one painting, so I looked and looked
as if to store it, and still,

as before, the figure of the girl
arrested me—not Flora with her flowers
or Venus or the Graces, who all seem
bored, including Mercury—but the girl,
panicked, being lifted by the blueish
angel in the trees, who isn't
an angel but the wind.

And what I'd never noticed were his wings.
Four long feathers gleaming
in the orange grove.
They resembled bean pods, or catalpas
that rattle in a breeze when they dry up.
Or four blue swords shining,
taking the girl to her fate.

How could I not have seen?
(The younger me, that is,
with my hip cocked, pausing for an
intellectual moment, headed for Greece
where I'd eat honey on the coast—
        is the future real, my son once asked—
            oh yes, oh yes)

This time I turned
to find my husband
in the crowd,
and I squinted at the opposite wall.
A new painting hung there, or
rather, an old one, restored in the years
between my visits, an "Annunciation"
(there are so many),

but in this one by Botticelli,
the angel has green wings,
luminous as infant grass
or a lily's elongated bud,
holding all that
shimmers inside.
I told my husband of the wings,

the death wings, and the birth wings
that reminded me of the Hopkins line
"There lives the dearest freshness
deep down things" —
but in those moments of waking
it's as if an angel comes to you
because no one else can hear.

The Matter

I have no memories of your father on the patio
in the morning, cornering the sick possum
in the chill of August on Cape Cod,
or of me wearing red lipstick to be alluring
for the houseguests;
I have no memories of our cocktailed odes
to Bursa, circumnavigation
or the South of France
that turned to squabbles
at the children's bedtime hour
in the darkening, mosquito-starred yard;
more than the night of your conception
I believe in your being born, with shoulders curving
wide and hard, guitar-like,
my stuck and turning son—
more than the stories I love the stubborn fact of you,
though later on the ward, the matter settled,
I thought,

I have always loved the word guitar.

One a.m.

Freight cars creak by in the dark
behind the yard.
Our son snuffles with a first cold.
One a.m. I've finished work.
Waking up these days, I lapse
back, as with one arm
flung for the first backstroke
to the water of dreams, whole stories.
The nightlight's glow, an urge to kiss you—
they're too soft,
remnants, shaken off.

Fortune

My fortune said,
"Let your natural versatility keep you from being bored."

I broke apart in a kind of despair
because my husband said—

but it didn't matter because one of us kept going.
They say now that the patient known as Sybil

didn't have sixteen personalities.
But I'm sure she did and we wanted her to—

at least one of us did, in Moroccan pajamas, an odalisque
thinking of Matisse (his arched doorways) and the valuation of
    decorative art.

I broke apart in a kind of despair because my husband said—
and then he asked,

Is it going to rain, my collarbone hurts again
(the memories like injuries recur:

Talking Heads, linoleum squares, bottles of beer
and we were there—a sibilance across years

of cold glass and dancing),
my collarbone hurts again, a yoke.

I broke apart in a kind of despair because my husband said—
and on my hand I saw, a ring around the bone.

Annunciation

Green rush of wings.
Green rush of wings
(grass and a hummingbird beating)
as he lands to tell her.
Outside, a castle in the distance
settles on a hill.
A stone bridge
spans the soft river.
While the window frame
gives serenely onto the view
a disturbance of wings
and tangled curls and
red robes
has entered the room.
He holds a lily.
He kneels as if fearing a blow.
Beyond his head, a window box
full of dirt and no flowers.
As she demurs, her stylized
hands push the messenger back.
Even as her head
bends to him to say yes.

Rain in Mexico

The day it rained in Mexico
Pierre appeared
at our door with beers
to celebrate & we got wet
standing on our motel-style
stone walkway
at leaf level for the grapefruit tree
& only then realized
how dry we'd been.
The dial telephone
outside by the shelf
full of thrillers in English
sometimes rang for us
& one night Tom killed
an arched scorpion (so sexual,
it wheeled backwards
in high heels
under the couch)
& we had a broom
but Tom had killed a snake
in India with a stone
so he came & then Doris.
They wanted us to learn bridge.
They'd been twenty years
out of country
& she talked at us all day long
which was friendly in a place of exile
but we didn't write to her after.
Their Krishnamurti tapes played
at low volume for hours
across the courtyard
were rain to us.
Darkness was rain
& our friends
calling to say they would come soon,
all of us just married.
Pierre waved from the opposite roof
when we all hung laundry

on top of our stucco apartment building
in a valley
between dry hills, and wringing out
pants in the deep sink
then smoothing them on the line
made me feel real
& Pierre with sturdy legs
& loose khaki shorts & wire glasses
looked like an old Peace Corps guy,
not a retired Canadian grocer.
Señora had us pay more
to have another room unlocked
for our friends,
who wore colored ankle socks
with lace-up shoes like Pierre did
& they were all born in Canada.
The beers were nice.
We & Pierre had the chat
about what brought us all here
& I'm sure we agreed
Señora was greedy & the man who fixed things
was a good man, the maid was inexpensive
& the dog would rip a throat out if he got loose.
Every day we had our outings,
to buy coffee or manchego cheese
at the state store
as Doris advised,
bread at a particular bakery,
books from the library,
laundry detergent or stamps
or beer,
fruits & vegetables from mounds
at the covered market,
a newspaper at the square
to keep up with the goings-on:
the striking schoolteachers
who camped for days,
Juarez's one hundred and eighty-fifth
birthday fireworks celebration,

the outdoor displays of porn magazines
& vaccination tables set up for babies.
I felt vaccinated
against being there, the abacus
of Spanish words I knew
& the rented apartment
my protection.
Sometimes young men wanted to practice
their English on us in the square,
where pregnant women strolling
all wore the same
type of dress,
in pillowcase pastels
with smocking over the breasts
and a Peter Pan collar.
I so much wanted a child.
There were four movie theaters
to go to, and a ruined city
where you could drink a Coke
under a tree
after admiring the bas-relief
carvings of fallopian tubes
and cesarean section.
I wish we could do it again
sometime—take off and stare at things,
happy not to know
why tents were raised, soup ladled,
the bowls smashed afterward on cobblestones,
or why colored candies and purses
appeared on carts one day
in the square, or why leaving
was what we were doing,
riding a silver bus to the mountains,
further south,
where people in hot-pink fabrics
emerged from forests above the fog.

Wedding

The day is here whitely proclaiming.

Alone, hiding a little from myself
    what I know.

In the fluid now
orange-throated birds hop
lizards ripple up the bark
a scorpion glides like a wedding train along the floor
    looking for a dark place
      a small inside, invisible stinging
(there are thousands of me, of me).

There is taking a bath in the wind
its arms and combs and beaters
the air being teased out & missionary
    black flies tossed
      & fruit flies gently bumping into vases.

There are speckles within speckles
    on the fruit.
A tree drops pale slippers—
when was I ever the one, or you?

I can't stop filling the spaces
    of you with implications
until the two of us are a mind
busy murdering what won't belong.

In Bed

I can't stop talking about the weather.
You say not to, and I can't stop.
Did they say it would rain?
The white light pours down—I don't
think it will rain, but did they say?
I don't know. It's eight o'clock
in the morning—
one child has a fever
and another is in a play about death
and nobody's slept.
He's performing all the parts about death,
death itself and the one who doesn't want to die.
The rain and the one who waits
for what they say—
they didn't call for snow sometimes they're wrong
it's no wonder with all this
change in weather he has a fever.
You say not to, and I can't
stop the white light that filters in
through fabric blinds.
If only you would with your hand
cover my mouth, lay down some violence
like what we watch with satisfaction on TV—
lay down some violence against me
while we wait for
death and what they say we'll get.

Book of Hours

Leaves like miniature red scythes or boomerangs scattered.
An apple peel spirals off the blade.
The tears of Republican women as they clutch in gold-buttoned suits.
The you of you coming home, smoke out of the scorched air.
A sheet corner sprouts like a fleur-de-lis into the room.
The touching, the folding like a triptych shut, the sightless pleasure.
The child growing larger by the hour, as if birth were endless.
She traps her small flying hand with her mouth.

Problematics of Early Modern Biography

One must not lard every page
with *maybes* and *perhapses*.

One must authorize a past,
unwritten, gapped.

So if you, forefather, came with a king
in 1660 as his soldier

on a ship from Scheveningen to Dover,
one must know it.

Here at night on the New England shore
coldness hisses on the stones—

like Scheveningen, with its dead
gel man-o'-war in blue, where I stood as a kid

shivering by the closed amusement pier,
eating French fries from a cone—

here a bonfire burns, and my little son
points at a star & says *superfire*.

Your son born during the Great Fire
of London was misplaced in the fearful

evacuation to the hills, then found
by his mother who

spied him in a neighbor's window,
his chin imperious with sorrow.

Your coat of arms is a greyhound. Or
three Dutch skates and a bloody hand.

You became British, or returned to Holland,
were made baronet, named Governor

of the Bahama Islands, or rather
of an uninhabited lesser one

you never visited. You fly across oceans
by satellite for us.

Far more of us
than the fifty thousand who lined the beach

to watch the royal fleet depart
or you, in an olive cape and boots,

sail into seamless time.

Elsewhere

I felt the rain hiss past
and revive the dead lavender.
Mums are thirsty, she said,
and my mother planted
them all around the house
and after school
I had to water them.
I felt the rain hiss past
and solidify.
Red beads of apples
fortify the countryside,
and early ginger golds,
which remind me of the lemons
on Italian trees
or the grass of sunlit
uplands, sloping isolated
in substations of the Alps.
My dream is elsewhere.
Hawks, he said, are good here,
though I've not been birding
in Pennsylvania.
I'm a tropical ornithologist.
Everyone spoke
of the crusty bread the baker makes—
not the usual squishy bread of town—
how they would run down a colleague
to get there first;
the bread is scarce.
Birds, you know, interest us
and yet we don't think of them
until we talk to you
and then not again either
until we think of you
or until the gang of cowbirds,
starlings, and grackles
that strings itself from

one side of town
to the other
knots down in our trees
and we wake to hissing
and their greasy cries.

Near the Turn of the Century

Near the turn of the century a great war began.
It was as if we had opened the next heavy volume.
There were servants, and pirates, and pain in the pelvic region.

A detective said, I need the name of every guest at the gala.
Wine came in boxes, and then it didn't, and then it did again.
She wrote to her children, a note on an index card. Dear Children,
    I want to tell you, the war has begun.

Or something like that. They drank the wine however it came.
Fighter planes flew low over the riding ring.
A man spread open a heavy book on his lap or a woman, his hands
    flat on the pages on the softest inner thighs he had ever known.

Pipilotti Rist made a film of a woman swinging a red-hot-poker flower
    and smashing car windows.
She had an anxiety attack between the flannel sheets.
She had the softest inner thighs he had ever known a long time ago.

They were waiting for them to say that the war had begun.
When it happened I was in Cala Foods buying arugula.
I was in a bookstore and they said bombs were dropping over there.

When should we have more coffee she said lazily in the flannel
    bed and he said let's have a divorce but he didn't say it
so they had coffee and washed their clothes again.
She hoped the play about death went really well for their child.

The Gaze

My child's long hair springs out of its confinements,
    out of pink elastics,
a golden furze around her face; at end of day, a haze
    above her hazel eyes
which slide from side to side as her pencil writes
    of salamanders, with their soft,
dolphin-like skin.

Her words, which sprout syntactically correctly,
    are salamandrine limbs
to move the body forward; she and Maria filled their hands
    with orange salamanders
which they set swarming on an island of moss.
    The girls and their wild
hair in the woods,

the girls in the wild wood
    where we walk in measured paces, watching them.
What did she know of salamanders
    before beginning her report? *I knew that they are usually
small.* Small enough to nest
    in tangled hair, as in my sister's, once,
when we were small.

People often mistake a newt for a salamander
    that they are "raising."
The newt will never grow. My child springs
    from her confinements.

Landscape

It's an attention disorder, seizing onto
what enters the frame:
black-eyed Susans, a margarine
clump by the driveway, their

protruding centers, and then
the next absorption—helping my son into
a plastic car, one of his arms
awkward with a vinyl purse.

Later it's perusing fake parchment currency
in lettered sets
for a nephew studying the Civil War.
There's a battlefield map,

too, and a copy of the Gettysburg Address,
Lincoln's script reproduced,
tucked into an envelope at Walmart,
where we go a lot of mornings

in our town. I like the people, our passion
for the best barrettes and school shoes,
the way we operate in a daze of tiredness:
I wish I'd bought that one,

the lawnmower sales associate says,
It's got a mulcher, chops the grass
into bits and puts it back into the ground.
My daughter's yelling, Don't

cut the grass mommy you'll kill it,
while he continues imperturbably on:
But I bought that one, with larger wheels, for my hills.

Though a world-famous skater lost, as a child,
half her foot to a mower, we must mow.
If she hadn't lost, she wouldn't be a star.
I like the way our diminishments

drive us toward a warped perfection.
The way everyone has a story:
causatives reel us here, where we are caught,
in a soft-focus August

out of which figures delineate against a ground.
We float: rest on surfaces, distinguished as ourselves.
And we form: ground bits and smears of landscape—
these shedding maples, those water-wrecked

abandoned stores across the lot,
petals almost unattached from flowers—gather us in.

Deer

There is no subject.
Or the subject sits like a clot,
or stripped nasturtium stems,
white ghost-roots in the garden.

The ones who eat the garden
come at night
for peppery velvet flowers
in the dark—I remember

the insinuating bougainvillea
that pinkly twined and curled
in Mexico, our ordered house,
us wandering amidst the luna-colored drinks

& aqua bars behind louvers,
comic books and fireworks,
like nocturnal dazzled animals—
I let them eat.

At the International School

She kept looking at the small bad picture from Nicaragua.
At the international school
the children of assassins and pornographers
ran zigzag in the courtyard.
The clouds like macaroons
stuck onto the flat sky.
(You must try the macarons at Ladurée,
the women said.) She kept falling
out of her class,
up or down, pasted onto
the background, wearing an appropriate purse.
At the international school
the children of assassins and pornographers
ran in bright clothes, shouting in Spanish
while their bodyguards idled in black Mercedes.
They waited so patiently
with black accessories, sunglasses and cell phones
and guns, a weakness for the primitive.

Dark Wood

My daughter is older now—
she won't be taken from me.
She is solid, real.
With Botticelli hair she swims in the forest still.
Once, morphine flew her through the dark.
Her eyes closed against the dark wood of the world.
(Here, this is what you must enter through—
a long blackness of harsh breathing,
being summoned to a far, daylit field.)
The forest is attached to her.
Sometimes she falls back in—
succumbing to convulsions,
her limbs in a filmy, suffocating garment.
Mother, father,
don't make me come out—
with wide hazel eyes
and a panicked, sideways glance—

Ledge

Sister and I
    stood on a ledge in white nightgowns.

A ledge like a narrow subway platform
    in a tunnel, tiled in ceramic
and barrel vaulted,
    as in London, where we once lived.

Instead of tracks, clear water.
    Instead of lights, flames on long sticks
projecting from the wall.
    Tiles shining, water clear, flames bright.

To either side, where the station ended, dark tunnel.
    We stared at the water
with a gasoline-sharp sense of a menace behind us.
    (Where to go?)

Our father,
    wanting to tell us a story.
About a maid, or his mother?
    Burning.

She was a demon, he is saying,
    and her dress, or the suggestion of one
burned up
    right in front of me,

and now he is pulling us
    through a dark, arched doorway.

Proofs

I spy for errors
in a high, windowed cubicle
in San Francisco.
I see ships roll by like buildings
in and out of harbor.
The processors type letters
on a screen, in green.
I hunt through a thicket
of innumerable crisp letters
for a misplaced *e*.

I knock humbly at a lawyer's door.
Excuse me, items one through nine
do specify the Foxes
liable for their loan.
(They've defaulted—now their boat,
house, facsimile machine will go.)
But item ten lists only Mr. Fox.
I lean on Jane the processor's desk
and say, Insert Mrs. Fox.
(I've asked for software
to replace me.)

In the temperate, windowless word room,
Jane resists becoming machine.
Some secretaries dress sexy, but Jane won't.
Others dress with the controlled allure
of flight attendants, or like mid-century college girls
in soft sweaters and pearls,
or stylish attorneys-to-be, but Jane will not.
She takes a hand-rolled cigarette
and smokes it in her carmine lips.
She has a narrow nose, an erect neck.
She wears part of a Mexican basket

in her hair, harem pants, black socks
and shoes, a sleeveless purple sheath.
I don't know how
she is allowed.

She is a processor in the process
of becoming Polish trapezist,
or Alice B. Toklas.
Jane is an actor.
She enters a flock of letters
like a swan.

I wear nude pantyhose with the rest
and place myself, which means erasure,
in service of a language
that stiffens in preparation
to be of service to a bank.
Dear Mrs. Fox, I whisper,
I've caught you in the night of item ten,
escaping in your boat on whipped-creamy
seas to Rio, and by the letters of your name
I send you home again.

I am the afternoon proofreader,
making marks with green pen.
The morning proofreader uses blue.
When we salute each other at the change,
we plot our dream TV show,
L.A. Proofreader.
Proofreaders are the stars.
We make bold marks, send law clerks
to wash our sports cars.
One day, we strike the phrase "said property,"

we sneer at it in our British supercilious
proofreader's way.
The lawyers sweat over a substitute
while we go out for an oyster lunch
with wine, and the dark flirtation
that keeps the show top-rated.
We are first on the scene
at any language accident.
Then we sigh.

Don is off to Berkeley
to study Buddha for the afternoon.

Delete, delete, delete!
The little loops of ink
defoliate the page.
Oh, there goes the office manager's
sprayed array of butter-colored hair!
An inky noose lifts a lawyer
straight up from his chair.
A lycra-covered bicycle messenger
is lassoed round the ankle.
A loop in district court is swinging
a judge above his courtroom, and out,
down Market Street to drop him gently

on a China Ocean Shipping Company freighter.
A black speck
on the deck.
A lowercase *l*
swaying with the swells,
now blowing lightly overboard.

Walk Onstage

Jorie Graham said to wear red lipstick,
walk onstage with your voice at its highest pitch.

Use your red lipstick to keep from being bored.

Walk onstage cock your hip dare them.
She wore long hair Italian sweaters cigarettes and breasts

nervous hands in her hair, she wore cheekbones
and a fluttery heart.

She would suffer attacks of anxiety, philosophy—
huge clumps of words linked to other clumps

with dashes, film stills
trapped in alphabets and time

(because I can't just lob a fireball of consciousness at you
and you can't catch a giant fireball of me and contain me).

Or maybe Jorie Graham *could* lob a giant fireball
and the reader's brain would glow with it like the (inexplicably)

radiant health center building in the
small bad picture of Nicaragua.

Wear red lipstick in the plaza—
walk onstage screaming, or declaiming—

or when he is in you, the temple glowing broken open.

She Falls Back In

As if she could vanish into a hazel wood
from which sticks are cut
for beating or divining.
As if she might be flattened there,
in a perpetual suggestive inaction
in which flowers had just streamed
from her lips
into the forest turning brittle or full,
between a winter and fertility
all motion suspended
before, in a violent burst of consciousness
(How did Persephone return to earth?)
she slammed into the world again.

PART TWO

Black Space

There were black places of eclipse—
    black space, a slab of slate, a black river
    beside her body laid out flat

(preserving the lumbar curve), her body arched,
    riverine, out-of-self, away,
    the bright public body eclipsed

even as the white light poured down upon them.
    He carried her far—
    the uses of myth being numerous.

        "greener than grass
      I am and dead—or almost
      I seem to me."

Fragment 31 of Sappho, that is, translated by Anne Carson.
The black desk will swallow me whole.
    Swifts, the bits of black in flocks

plunge parabolic past stone walls
    into the dense ravine and up,
        over the medieval town built on a Roman drilling ground

        (one layer down, the altars made for sacrifice).
    Beside the rush of water, her body laid out curved on stone
    takes the form of supplication and consent.

What is a body against fingers of volcanic stone
    or sunlit upland fields of shale?
    She leaves and she remains.

Call

You're only as old as a cloud.
I heard
a voice out of blackberries, that old thicket
of the short thorns,
call me mother.
                            Mother, how
have you left me here?
In the sly needles
with only a stem to lick.
Don't not see me.
Call me the fruit.

Night

Some nights, time,
it seems, expands;
not like a dark containing
liquid, not quite
holding us in its invisible

hammock weave
but soft and potent, the way darkness
takes in the skunk
leaving for us only
its white flashing, like a revolving

tiny Milky Way, in transit
from one yard-universe
to another. We see the neighbors'
blue-changing televisions,
lit planet earths,

through zones
of the medium (where the dark
and the light meet,
our daughter says).
Our gestures flash like rings

between rooms
as we lock doors, draw shades,
wash the pans, talk of work.
I read the paper: still,
only minutes have passed.

An extragalactic pocket has
enveloped us, or time is
pregnant with space.
Time has bloomed,
like the cloud of parasols,

pink terraces,
in the perennial bed;
or branched, like water's

black narrative trickle
along the buried walls

of our house.
Sometimes when an argument
becomes thin, and
ridiculous,
a new tone,

rounder, like an hour
or a lamplit circle,
enters in.
Then our old voices scissor up
like burned paper, weightless & of the past.

River

There is a place where the grass
rolls down a narrow hill
and fans out like a pool.
There is a place where the girls

stare straight out
in old sweatshirts, with their hair
in clumps, and look poor.
A place where the bee pivots in dirt.

Where the roots are gray tendons.
Where the eyes see poorly,
and the mouth drinks.
Where the voice comes down a hallway

and smacks you.
Where the brown spiders hide
behind the washer, behind
the furnace.

Where the light falls feebly down
on mop streaks.
Where the yellowjackets rise
in electric clouds

into the air scaffolded
with blossoms.
Where the girls hold their kittens
on the fieldstone wall.

Where they look up through maple leaves
in ripped chiffon gowns
from Johnson's inaugural ball.
Where the mother watches them from.

Where the arrow-shaped stone
marks a property line.
Where the dog got hit and crippled.
Where the canal runs,

sluggish, opaque.
Where the towpath goes
its dusty way across states.
Where the Delaware runs wide and shallow,

ruffling over stones.
Where it deepens and browns.
Water snakes float,
black sticks,

and the swimmers wear tennis shoes.
Where the rabbit expired panting
and exhaling spills of blood
on the damp evening lawn.

Where the girls sat transfixed
in a circle and a carful
of cousins billowed past.
Where the factories drained.

Where the river caught fire
and men preserved in photographs
on the bungalow walls
fought it from the banks

with buckets
and watched tangled islands burn.
Where the islands went.
Where ashes fell.

Where grasshoppers spring sideways and disappear.
Where the praying mantis eats
the silently waving insects
and tilts its triangular face.

With a War On

Heels across the hardwood.
She peers at the picture.
A scarf of smoke is pinned to the volcano top.
The macaroon clouds are exhausted.
Stick figure dolls dance in the square.
You can't see
through the larval clumps of leaves.
You can't penetrate anything
in a small bad picture,
the church put on there like a sticker.

Circumstance

The world wanted her.
I cradled her across my lap.
The world wanted her
to stay in its rough circumstance:
but her breath fell, and her color fell away
as if something had taken
and turned her, the way a wind
reverses leaves,
to the verdigris unconsciousness
of before, before, before.
Awkwardly I carried her
up the hill to home.
Her legs dangled down.
Ungainly and tired from giving birth
to her brother,
I wished that I were stronger
to carry my girl in my arms
with a measure of dignity,
or shelter.

A Bavaria of the Mind

By the road, a nag eats plums in a field.
Mr. Schleg has left the camarilla;
he limps under the lemony trees.

He is a figurine of fear
for his children back at home, daddy nightmare
clanking lead-footed upstairs.

Once he lined up his children on the grass
with dark glasses bought for the eclipse
and one thought fiercely, *You can't blind this—*

and looked unprotected, an angel into the blaze.
In Bavaria, the citizens threw dolls into bonfires
and ate apples in the snow.

There, Mr. Schleg says, a pretender arose
while he was being born in America
and fell in a river, catching polio.

A cubist harlequin, Mr. Schleg,
he walks a two-faced, crumpling way,
whole and full and tall on his left leg,

down on his right, like a small building tilting,
with an involuntary crimp of his lips,
his cane stabbing and planting itself.

One of his selves drove to the office in a blue car.
The other jumped back into the alembic river,
emerging as the glittering long-lost heir

to the throne of Bavaria,
whose mother complained of nostalgia
as they strolled beneath the plane trees

whose branches had been severed
leaving bare, lumpy knobs for winter.
He bought an airline ticket

and found a country with the wrong name,
a horse with yellow teeth and mane,
plenipotentiaries who called him insane.

In an evening bath he lay morose
and cried, as lather and dirt iridesced,
for a sledge piled with otter pelts

hissing across the forest floor
of ancient towering firs,
for store-bought saplings held up with wires

on his one and a half-acre
suburban lot in Pennsylvania,
and soapily sank into mania.

Mr. Schleg lived in our neighborhood that spread like moss
muffling the assembled sounds, softening,
and drank cocktails

in neighbors' backyards with citronella,
gently spiraling plumes of seductive
smoke uncoiling.

Verge

There is the shopping center.
We walk there to steal
small things, smoke cigarettes.
I am twelve.
There is a reason for walking
an hour along the canal
to Calhoun Street, the iron bridge,
metal-signed shopping center
where storefronts glare silver
against pavement.
Where we steal
what we don't even want,
I finger plastic orange earrings in a bin,
stand on cracked tiles.
In the cool store, dust
settles on the merchandise,
identical objects in heaps.
I know so little,
I think the boys who make pizza
flirt with me
spinning aluminum pans on one finger.
I wear a halter top, I smoke menthol
cigarettes, I don't know yet
about inhaling.
The iron bridge leads to Trenton
over the muddy Delaware;
cars stop at a light
before they surge over the river.
I walk barefoot
on metal grating, read the sign
on the next bridge down,
TRENTON MAKES THE WORLD TAKES.
I hold my earrings.
The department store will shut down soon,
and the world will take us,
childhood closing its doors and registers,
our stolen treasures in our hands.

Wedding, Night

Heels are glamorous, for Ingrid of Mallorca
perusing Louboutins on a mirrored carousel
in the Paris boutique
after a prix-fixe lunch at Ladurée
    (the macarons in rose and gold,
        tied up in boxes).

Much later on Mallorca,
nets of lights constellate the olive trees,
a handsome stranger bearing flutes of cava
sidles by the swimming pool.
Ingrid the bride is beautiful and more,
illuminated, the picture of health, retaining mysteries—
    penetrable yet unseen.

The celebrants dance in a fire-lit cave,
and their heels do not hurt them.
They stumble drunken down a mountain road
    calling out to one another, finding no one—
  they might fuck in a ditch at this point—
blazing lonely stars burning solitary curlicues in the dark, wild space
    before they are gathered and bundled, village-bound.

Ingrid is married now.
She strides across the hardwood in heels.
I think she's beautiful.
I clump across the floor, preserving mysteries,
    hoping for a costume change behind the larval jacarandas—

    in the vast space between this self and another one.
    Sybil flashed from self to self in a shutterclick a breath,
what seductive possibilities she had
    beaten into her.
Whole in body, fractal mind.
    From a cave, the sibyl's voice flies multiple as swifts.

In the Exhibit

We saw a painted Mary,
not holding her son
but waiting to.
In the dim upstairs exhibit
of carved, dwarf-sized statuary
made of fruitwood
three centuries before,
this is what I wanted:
stories that lasted.
As to why this was the story
of our lives
people believed in
I could not tell her.
In a darkness so gathered, enfolding
and old, beneath the cathedral ceiling;
in a darkness so deliberate
and scripted,
dusted with the residue of ink, and smoke.
The dead Christ polychrome with blood.
Diminutive Mary, hands pinned to her sides
as if she would be helpless
even to receive him.

Asylum

Why don't we
break out of here.
We're standing in a cornfield,
chopped and cleared.

It's a chilly afternoon.
Low buildings hum behind us.
A sedan with perfect shocks
whispers past like the moon.

The road is tantalizing as a river
with a last, tree-lush bend.
You point your cigarette
at the invisible.

Why don't we walk along the road.
We're seventeen and wayward.
The juvenile boys' home is two miles down,
two miles past our boundary line.

The good kids drive there
once a week
to teach the bad ones basketball.
That's about the place where

you drove a tractor into a wall.
I pretended I didn't
exist yet.
But then I swallowed a jarful.

Why won't the doctor
ask me about sex?
It's a long road, and sparse farms.
The boys who run away never get very far.

You crashed a car and then you crashed
your father's tractor.
He made you cultivate his fields.
There's a smell in the woods here

that comes in when it likes.
White nightclouds float by.
It enters through window glass,
seeps, you can't keep it away.

Loretta S.—don't
laugh at this—drowned when we were twelve
in the cesspool of an abandoned house.
It's that smell.

She had coarse long hair,
uncut, tied back with kitchen string.
Why don't we just break
out of our minds?

When you hit the wall,
all the birds you threw rocks at
and cursed at, cowbirds and crows
and blackbirds, flew up in your face.

The doctor twirls his chair around.
I get an eyeful of upholstery.
Why don't we play guitar and smoke.
The oak trees going to ghosts.

I know we lined up in the gym
and the doctor said, Clap!
And only you and I clapped.
We follow all the rules until we get it.

Arc

Joan turns her armored chest toward you.
She says:

I was burning
when they came for me to burn me.

Her breastplate gathers to a point, it points
at her chin.

How controlled, how symmetrical she is
in a mildewed bedroom over crooked streets.

No, there is a collision, there is hair and sweat,
she is in disorder, no one has yet said

what she'll keep and what she'll tell
of a forest theater of voices.

She is still plastic,
her feet bleed

as they drag her over the oval stones,
each with its oval shine.

She is still a mess, the story has not dressed her
for the hole yet, in Christ on his globe

and golden lilies on a white satin field.

In the Village

I thought I would be whole but I won't be.
The secrets make dark pockets of space
and down that way around a corner
in the walled village
a couple is coupling on a stone floor
(yeah, sure, like train cars, chain links,
doing the mystery dance),
the marrieds are making espresso
and the dotty British widow waters her flowers
while a drunken man leans out a window
bellowing like a sea lion
and the bottleglass sea far below us all
winks and hisses.
There is blood on the stone street
from a boy falling flat, there is vomit
from a carsick girl, and there is a mother
washing it away with a rush of water
and lord knows what all is on the street
from cats and birds from time
out of mind before and after the earthquake
the plague the wars.

Primavera

Who is she, in the in between,
a not-yet Flora
(predictably dispensing roses,
summoning the bees).
She is the only one discontent,
flailing as gray hands pull her from behind
to erase her,
the girl,
transforming her into a goddess.
(More finished, more self-sufficient.)
I stood in the Uffizi once, before the painting
with the other young travelers.
Looking at it, I looked at her,
the one not settled yet.
And who calls me now, these years later
but Chloris,
the one in metamorphosis,
the daughter-girl.
She calls on me for this: to see her there.
A mother as witness
to a girl and her disappearance
into radiance, unconsciousness
or the subsequent
version.

Winter in France

All the heads ache in a sharp December cold.
The assistant, lonely for his artist,

carries a market basket
and, on his arm,

the artist's tiny trembling dog with bulging eyes,
hyper and overbred.

Like a black orchid corsage
worn to a dance in the gym.

Snow advances to the hills surrounding town.
The artist, who has touched lepers in India, returns.

"The point is not to cure them,"
he says, pouring wine.

Massaged into a state of grace
one might lift her cotton veil

and have an ordinary conversation.
At night he feeds his chickens in their cage

in the rain. The many eyes pricked with light
look out, glossy as caviar.

Someone always burns trash in the valley.
Smoke forms a column, its little black aspects

float into town.
There are well-dressed widows who tend

the upright cypresses, which stand
like candles on the hill.

I Am the Elder

I am the elder
who gets superseded

by a gold cross on a hillside,
the blue sea divided.

I ate the red seeds and the pits.
I could wear a necklace for protection,

turn my body into a city-state,
or a delicate and varied landscape,

greedy for attention.
Some weeds wave silver paws in the sun.

Why is the long hair caught in his lips,
why is her pallor romantic?

Why is someone sturdy not marching
across the square to save us?

Lay Down Some

"and on a soft bed
delicate
you would let loose your longing"
let loose like smoke or water, fire or perfume
infinite and dissipating.
That's why the small bad picture of Nicaragua
is all wrong—
every element has edges.
The smoke is stuck to the volcano,
not mingling with air.
The volcano smokes and heats nothing.
The children make no sound
while their parents clean their guns
part their lips in preparation
as the white light pours down upon them
in white studio spaces
high in suburban hills above the sea.
The sea glitters and swallows Icarus.

"into desire I shall come"
and come, a flame-flower, named
Tritoma, thrice-cut.
Use me to smash windows, break open
vehicles, forms and clinics;
release the zigzag energy,
the lava bullets blossoms molten gold.
Lay down some.
I am moving through an arched
doorway in a fever of white light
with the natural versatility of Sybil
let loose—
Violate me by the river you know you want to
lay down some by the river in me.
The making of art is about breathing.
Your breath on me and mine on you.
We are that close.
So break me open and bear me away.

Trompe L'oeil

is what the region's famous for —
Madonna in a niche on
the cathedral façade
being actually flat paint, or
stone window frames that aren't.
The children disappearing
around corners
of the crooked-packed medieval
houses, with a flash
of white sock or blue shoulder,
pale squeak of sneaker.
Or they come out, preceded by
an orange plastic arrow,
shouts, a fusillade of steps —
they're here, dimensional
until the stones and feline shadows
take their places.

Slip

The past is never past.
It just keeps coming back.
He's always getting drunk.
He's always saying, *your mother*
        in an angry tone.
Father's always drunk in the dark
        and we're holding hands
Trying to slip into the forest,
        mayflowers at our ankles.

We're always swimming up
        the Delaware River
So the current won't carry us down
        (Why not just go?).
Washington is always crossing it
        to surprise the troops at Trenton.
He's always pointing ahead
        with his nose and the prow.
They're always cleaning up
        the cannon with that Q-tip.
Ahead, he says, Cross the river.

But it's always 1776.
It's always 1972.
We're always wearing white nightgowns.
He's always saying, *let me*
        tell you a story
In a confiding tone
And the story will always destroy us.

A Rush of Light

She was fussing with her face,
trying to pop an imperfection
and it wasn't going well.
Have you ever had that happen to you?

Have you had everything happen to you?
Have you been entered by the river, called
Guinevere, drunk too much done coke
with the boss, polished your weapon,

worn thigh-highs taken down
your hair and crawled
as the hot light poured down upon you?
The babysitter and her best friend danced

in a suburban living room to classical music,
fingertips touching in an arched bridge,
heels not touching the hardwood floor,
weaving a scarf of invisible smoke

between them, she remembers.
Did they wear white flowing dresses,
crowns of flowers?
Light streamed in through panes,

through the green, wild space
of overgrown backyard,
through leaves, through air particled
with factory smoke,

a rush of light fell on them
while two girls as if
in the wings sat watching.

Crown

The horse against the sun
is lined with fire.
My daughter rides her
western-style,
heels down,
hips easy in the saddle.
She used to toss her head
when she kicked that reddish horse—
a flourish, an italic
emphasis.
Now she tilts her face
up steadily, and the sun
gilds her laughing,
wheeling around the ring
in figure eights.
The sun sinks on spindles.
An old goose
cranks from the far field.
I see the body radiant
as a November day shuts its gate—
girl and horse a thin corona
before the fence.
Before the twilight cold
begins, and
banks and fractures us.

Springtime

Trains blowing through the dark.
Flowers to the south
side of the house roused and slackened.
The carnival arrives
across the street. Men test the lights—
bars of pink and white,
The Hustler in blue script.

Killer Dream

I was going to Killer Island, a small island,
mid-river.
There were so many bridges over the river,
crossing each other at various heights
in the morning commuter dark—
black ironwork and lights rushing through,
like strips of film held arched over the river—
it seemed sci-fi, futuristic,
the industrial age gone manic.
Yet the scene also resembled the Susquehanna
at Harrisburg, Pennsylvania,
which it was,
with its plethora of bridges,
its cheap amusement park, City Island,
its papery—as a wasp's nest is—twin
nuclear reactors set round the bend mid-river.
I rode backwards in a high train,
seeing the treasure-boxes lit,
the privacies revealed.
Silhouettes drank coffee in river mansions
so grandly renovated they seemed empty,
their original inhabitants
now in the cemeteries
we use as landmarks.
A vendor presided over a shop
full of paperbacks and stamps,
newspapers and tickets, all
in the washed pastels of European
bills, his shop hulking
on its island in a squat.
On the receding bank, deciduous trees
hung heavy, leafy in June,
and the gold dome of the capital shone roseate
in the rising light—
suddenly the river could have been
the Delaware at Trenton & I a different,
former person,
citizen of a different river.
It was a destabilizing moment.

I had an appointment
where once a murderer had worked,
in a buzzing sort of fury, or fission,
and the vendor in his shop, hands flexed
on his apron pockets, red-faced, looked
murderously up at me.
I feared anyone could kill anyone,
each of us a small, contained explosion.

Dream

When our daughter's eyes open
as we kneel
time starts again; time starts
again for us,
vigilant at a birth.
We might be statues, stilled
in the twirl of dust.
Her eyes flick, side to side;
she can't remember where
she's come from.
Once it was morning on the sofa—
her skin and the light
had a pale celery cast.
Once it was Christmas, amidst
the crumpled wrappings.
All the roses gone,
and a long, whitefaced journey back.
As an infant, her eyes were like a seer's—
a glassy indigo, still of the dark
unphysical dream—
We dimmed the lights.
We would entice her to us.
To our cycles of planting seeds,
cutting flowers, tending
our gardens made
dormant and lustrous by ice.

He Turned the Woman into a Tree

He turned the woman into a tree.
She wasn't doing anything for the painting
so there she went
near the turn of the century with a war on.

She walked along a city street
in a sky-blue dress swinging a long stem
laying down some violence
with a poker-flower and auto glass.

In the small bad picture of Nicaragua
the tree-leaves beetled together for warmth,
their eyes invisible underneath,
blue exoskeletons shaped like shields.

A woman appeared at the lower left door
of a white church, her back to it.
She wasn't going in, and she was doing
a lot for the black-and-white photograph,

providing contrast and tension
and the suggestion of sex or sex withheld
which is what the pornographers have all wrong
in their white studios where the promises are kept.

You push a button and the volcano smokes
and heats nothing.
The woman moans but does not writhe,
her hair remains untangled and a river

would be expensive.
She walks down to the river and steps in
lifting the hem of her white dress,
her hair falling like weeping branches.

A woman smokes in a doorway, looking out
at dense undergrowth sits on the undergrowth
in a picnic dress retrieves groceries sits on
the marriage bed in front of a pocked wall.

They're all the same woman, the uses
of myth being numerous as flowers, bones, assassins
or small bad pictures that have no
breathing underneath.

I Meant to Speak

I meant to speak only of angels,
yet they resemble so much else—

white sails approaching port, or
migratory birds returning,

sheets shook out on a balcony,
two hands, a swan,

the snowy cape
of a plague inspector, his paper

beak stuffed full of flowers,
knocking at houses

for the hidden blackened ones.
I meant to speak only of fortune—

I once was sure and certain
as a stone

      (or the way that sounds)

my body yet to multiply
and wander.

Notes

The epigraph's three lines are quoted, but not attributed, in *Vence: Immortal Village* by Donald Culross Peattie (Chicago: The University of Chicago Press, 1963). They are from the opening lines of "Mignon's Song," a poem in Goethe's novel *Wilhelm Meister's Apprenticeship.*

The title of "Small Bad Picture" alludes to, and the poem directly refers to, the poem "Large Bad Picture" by Elizabeth Bishop, from her collection *North & South* (1946), and included in *Elizabeth Bishop: The Complete Poems, 1927-1979* (New York: Farrar, Straus and Giroux, 1983).

In "The Visit," the quoted line is from Gerard Manley Hopkins's poem, "God's Grandeur."

The last line of "The Matter" is the first and last line of David St. John's poem "Guitar" in his book *The Shore* (Boston: Houghton Mifflin Company, 1980). The poem itself pays homage to his poem, using its phrasings and rhythms with different content; the second and third lines of St. John's poem are, for example, "I have no memories of my father on the patio / At dusk, strumming a Spanish tune . . ."

In "Fortune," the patient known as Sybil was Shirley Ardell Mason, diagnosed in 1954 with dissociative identity disorder, then known as multiple personality disorder. Her story was told in the 1973 book *Sybil* by Flora Rheta Schreiber, and then in a popular 1976 television miniseries, starring Sally Field and Joanne Woodward, for which Field won an Emmy.

"In Bed" alludes to the play *Death Knocks* by Woody Allen, originally published in *The New Yorker,* July 27, 1968.

"Problematics of Early Modern Biography" was the title of a scholarly panel session at an MLA conference.

The film described in "Near the Turn of the Century" is Pipilotti Rist's audio video installation, *Ever Is Over All,* 1997, on view in the late nineties at MOMA in New York.

The last lines of "Landscape" allude to *Float and Form,* a 1996 painting by Richard Baker.

In "Black Space," Sappho's fragment 31, from which the three quoted lines are excerpted, appears in *If Not, Winter: Fragments of Sappho,* translated by Anne Carson (New York: Knopf, 2002). "Lay Down Some" depends on the same source; the quoted lines are excerpts from, respectively, Sappho's fragments 94 and 96, as translated by Carson.

"Slip" has in mind the 1851 painting, *Washington Crossing the Delaware*, by Emanuel Leutze, a copy of which hangs in the visitors' center at Washington Crossing, Pennsylvania. A stone marker by the river there reads, "Near this spot Washington crossed the Delaware on Christmas night 1776. The eve of the Battle of Trenton." The crossing is reenacted twice every December at the Washington Crossing Historical Park.

In "He Turned the Woman into a Tree," the images of women in the fourth, seventh, and eighth stanzas allude to photographs by Cindy Sherman in her series, *Untitled Film Stills*, 1977-80.